The Usborne
ART BOOK
about
Portraits

Rosie Dickins

Illustrated by Elisa Paganelli
Designed by Nicola Butler

Let's look inside...

D1638110

National Galleries
of Scotland

In association with
The National Gallery,
London

National Portrait Gallery,
London

Contents

Usborne Quicklinks

For links to websites where you can see lots more portraits
and try creating your own, go to www.usborne.com/quicklinks
and type in the title of this book. Please read our internet
safety guidelines at the Usborne Quicklinks website.

The picture opposite is a close-up of *Portrait of the actor
Nakamura Shikan V;* turn to page 25 to see the whole image.

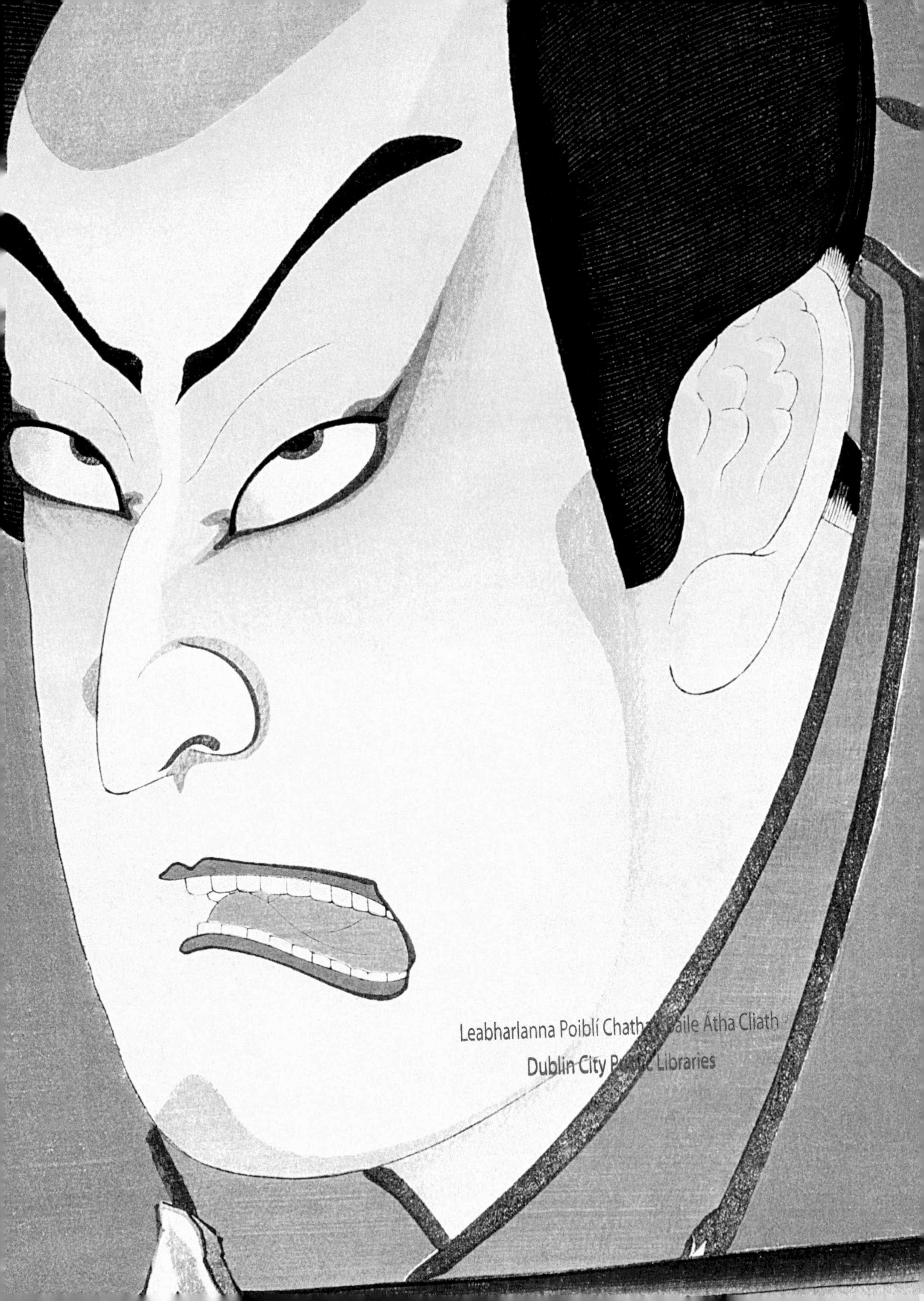

All over the world, and across the centuries, artists have chosen to paint and sculpt and photograph images of people. You'll find lots of different examples of them in this book.

This portrait was made as a 'tronie' or study of an expression. We don't even know the name of the girl who posed for it.

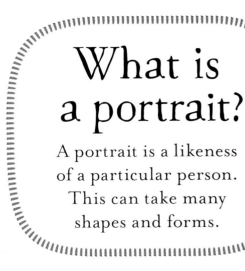

What is a portrait?

A portrait is a likeness of a particular person. This can take many shapes and forms.

Girl with a Pearl Earring
by Johannes Vermeer, about 1665

This miniature portrait was worn on a chain like a jewel, to remember a loved one.

Sir Walter Ralegh
by Nicholas Hilliard,
about 1585

Before photography, the only way to preserve a likeness was to hire an artist – if you could afford to. Many artists made a living by painting portraits for the rich and powerful.

Pictures of artists by themselves are known as self portraits. These let artists experiment without having to please anyone else. For example, they might try out a new pose or materials, or new ideas about how to show someone's personality.

Frida Kahlo is famous for her frank self portraits. Here, she painted herself with a pet monkey, wryly noting their similarities.

Some artists have experimented with distorting mirrors, to show a face in a different way.

Self Portrait with Monkey
by Frida Kahlo, 1938

Today, the most common form of portrait is a photograph. This could be a casual snapshot or 'selfie', or a professional portrait – composed and lit as carefully as a painting.

Queen of Scots, Sovereign of the Most Ancient and Most Noble Order of the Thistle and Chief of the Chiefs
photograph by Julian Calder, 2010

This woman's head was carved around 24,000 years ago, when the world was still in the throes of the last ice age. It's one of the earliest known images of a human face.

Woman from Brassempouy by an unknown artist, about 24,000 years ago, found in Brassempouy, France

The carving – made from a woolly mammoth tusk – is smaller than your thumb.

Magical pictures

People have been making portraits for thousands of years. These early images seemed so powerful that some ancient people even believed they had magical properties.

This clay sculpture of a soldier was part of a vast army, built to guard the tomb of China's first emperor. Thousands of similar soldiers were found alongside him – each with a different face and hairstyle.

The soldiers were originally brightly painted and held real weapons.

Terracotta Soldier by an unknown Chinese artist, about 2,200 years ago (Terracotta is a kind of clay.)

Some of the most beautifully detailed early portraits come from ancient Egypt. This golden mask shows Egyptian pharaoh, Tutankhamun. It was placed over his mummy, to help preserve his remains for the afterlife.

Smooth, gold features give the pharaoh an unreal, god-like appearance.

The painting below was found on another Egyptian mummy. The man's features were painted with great care, to create a very lifelike, individual portrait.

Mask of
Tutankhamun
by an unknown
Egyptian artist, about
3,300 years ago

The mask and the man's wreath use real gold, showing how much the Egyptians valued these images.

A Man with a Wreath
by an unknown Egyptian artist, about 1,900 years ago

Some portraits show people not as they truly were, but as a kind of perfect version of themselves. This could have been a way of asserting their importance, since in ancient times perfection was thought to be a quality of the gods. This coin shows a Greek king, Alexander, with the smooth good looks of Apollo, the ancient Greek sun god.

Curly hair, youth, beauty and a wreath of laurel leaves were all traits of Apollo.

Alexander the Great as Apollo
gold coin from about 2,300 years ago

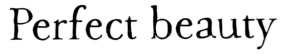

Perfect beauty

A portrait based on ideas about beauty and how the artist thought someone *should* look, rather than their actual appearance, is known as an 'idealized' portrait.

People have been creating idealized portraits since ancient Greek times. The statue on the left is an example. It was made to celebrate a chariot race winner – but the face is too smooth and symmetrical to be a true likeness.

Notice the calm expression and lack of wrinkles.

Charioteer of Delphi (detail of head and shoulders)
by an ancient Greek sculptor, about 2,500 years ago

This Italian painting of a young woman has been partly idealized. Notice her pale, smooth skin and calm expression. But her uneven nose and small chin are more individual, suggesting her features were painted more truthfully.

The profile view was inspired by ancient portraits such as those on coins.

It was fashionable for women to pluck their hair to make their foreheads higher.

The woman's name is not recorded, but the design on her sleeve was probably her family emblem.

Portrait of a Lady by Alesso Baldovinetti, about 1465

The portrait below was ground-breaking in its day. At the time, women were usually painted in profile – but this woman is shown looking towards us. It is among the earliest known examples of this pose in Italian art.

Ginevra de' Benci
by Leonardo da Vinci, about 1474-78

The painting is so detailed, you can see individual hairs.

Ginevra de' Benci

Leonardo da Vinci painted this portrait of a young Italian poet, Ginevra de' Benci, when she was just 16.

Leonardo included extra clues on the back of the painting, to help identify Ginevra. A prickly sprig of juniper refers to her name, which sounds like juniper (*ginepro*) in Italian. It is framed by more greenery and a scroll of praise.

The scroll reads, in Latin: 'Beauty adorns virtue' – praise for Ginevra's looks and character.

There's juniper on the front of the picture, too. A dark bush behind Ginevra frames and emphasizes her pale, delicate face.

Wreath of Laurel, Palm and Juniper with a Scroll
by Leonardo da Vinci, about 1474-78

The portrait wasn't originally square. At some point, the bottom was cut off, probably because it was damaged. The missing part would have shown Ginevra's hands, most likely folded in her lap a bit like this.

Warts and all

Some portraits present a surprisingly unflattering face to the world, often as a way of asserting how truthful or lacking in vanity they are.

Oliver Cromwell
by Samuel Cooper,
1656

The miniature portrait on the right shows English ruler, Oliver Cromwell. It records his thinning hair, wrinkles and warts with unflinching honesty. Cromwell was deeply religious and thought vanity was a sin; he wanted to be painted 'warts and all'.

An Old Woman
('The Ugly Duchess')
by Quinten Massys, about 1513

The painting on the left is a startlingly truthful portrait of an old woman with a disfiguring disease. She, in turn, inspired 19th-century artist and illustrator, John Tenniel, who turned her into a grumpy duchess for the book, *Alice in Wonderland*.

The Duchess and her Family
by John Tenniel, 1891
Notice the matching headdress.

The names of the man and child in this portrait have been lost, but tradition has it they are a man and his grandson. The artist deliberately contrasts the old man's worn, diseased face with the fresh face of the boy. Their embrace makes plain that age and appearance don't matter to them.

An Old Man and his Grandson by Domenico Ghirlandaio, about 1490

Most portraits began with someone hiring an artist. Then there would be several 'sittings' (meetings between artist and model) for the artist to make studies. This might take a few days, but sometimes much longer.

Study for a Portrait of Horace Walpole
by Allan Ramsay, about 1759

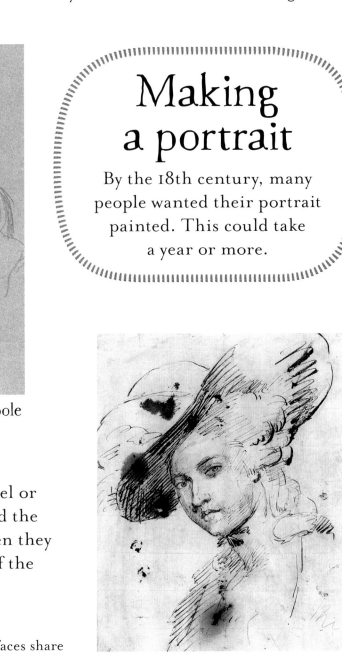

Mary Robinson
by Sir Joshua Reynolds, about 1782

Sir Joshua Reynolds used to offer his clients a selection of studies, so they could pick the one they liked best.

Making a portrait

By the 18th century, many people wanted their portrait painted. This could take a year or more.

Artists would often try the model or 'sitter' in different poses, to find the best or most flattering one. Then they would make careful drawings of the sitter's features.

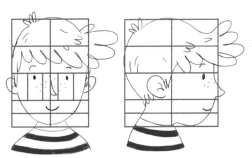

All faces share certain basic proportions, with the eyes about halfway down.

More drawings were made to plan out the clothes and background, often without the sitter being there. The artist's assistants might help out with these parts.

Thomas Gainsborough used wooden dummies when sketching clothes.

18th-century artist Joseph van Aken was so good at painting fabrics, other artists used to hire him to paint the clothes for them.

What a beautiful dress!

As in England almost everybody's picture is painted, so almost every painter's work is painted by Van Aken.

Horace Walpole

Once the layout of the finished picture was decided, it was copied onto a canvas. Before artists could begin painting, they had to prepare or 'prime' the canvas with a white or coloured underlayer.

Next came the paints. Turn the page to find out more...

Louise de Broglie, Countess of Haussonville
by Jean-Auguste-Dominique Ingres, 1842

...and now the paint

From the 16th century, most portrait artists used oil paints, as these allowed them to work slowly and capture subtle effects.

Until the 1840s, you couldn't buy tubes of paint. So artists made their own, using powdered colours known as 'pigments', made from crushed rock or plants.

Pigments were ground by hand, then blended with oil.

Artists often started by painting the face and hands. Sometimes, a busy artist might paint *only* the face and hands, leaving the rest to be completed by assistants.

Traditionally, artists would build up the paint in layers. They would begin by blocking out areas of light and dark, then gradually add colours in thin layers on top.

King George IV
by Sir Thomas Lawrence, about 1814

This unfinished portrait shows several different stages of applying paint.

This kind of underpainting, done all in lights and darks, is known as a 'grisaille'.

Oil paints take a long time to dry. So pictures would be left for around six months to 'cure'. Finally, the finished work was varnished to protect it.

A successful portrait could bring fame to both artist and sitter. After the painting below was exhibited, its artist was flooded with requests for similar portraits, and the woman it shows became celebrated as a society beauty.

Lady Agnew of Lochnaw by John Singer Sargent, 1892

Shah Jahan was an Emperor of India, famed for building a magnificent domed tomb known as the Taj Mahal. This lavish miniature painting shows him sitting on a golden throne, ringed by a golden halo – a symbol borrowed from western religious art – to emphasize his importance.

The Shah was fabulously wealthy and his throne was made of solid gold, studded with pearls and gems. This picture contains real gold too.

In real life, the picture is slightly smaller than shown here. It was originally displayed in an album.

Shah Jahan seated on the Peacock Throne
by Govardhan, about 1635

Kings and queens

For kings, queens and other rulers, a work of art was a way to display their power and project a certain image of themselves, like a kind of advertising.

The ancient kingdom of Ife in Africa, home of the Yoruba people, became known for its beautiful, natural-looking portraits of its royal rulers – such as this head of a queen, wearing a beaded crown.

Experts think the heads were probably used in royal rituals.

Head of a
Yoruba Queen
by an unknown African
artist, between 600
and 900 years ago

This portrait shows Princess Mary of England, eldest daughter of King Henry VIII, a few years before she became queen. Sumptuous clothes and jewels proclaim her high status. The artist used real gold and silver to add to the effect.

Gold letters in the background spell out the date plus Mary's name, age and family.

Mary I
by Master John, 1544

The Lacemaker by Johannes Vermeer, about 1669-70

Ordinary folk

From the 15th century, as a wealthy middle class sprang up, people besides kings and nobles began to have their portraits painted too.

Can you spot a book in the scene on the left? It's probably a Bible – a symbol of virtue.

The portrait on the left shows a woman weaving lace – a task requiring a lot of skill and patience. Her gaze draws attention to her busy hands. Her calm, hard-working air is meant to demonstrate her good character.

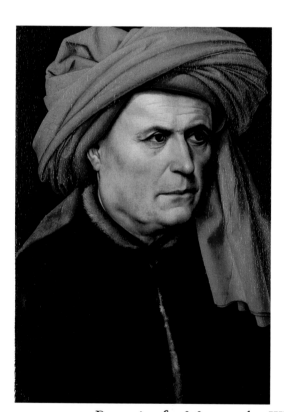

Portrait of a Man and a Woman by Robert Campin, about 1435
Plain, dark backgrounds let nothing distract from the faces themselves.

The two portraits above were made as a pair. The names of the sitters have been lost, but they were probably a married couple. Their plain, fur-lined gowns and headdresses show they were well-to-do but not nobles.

Some paintings put more emphasis on light and colour than clear shapes – such as Claude Monet's picture of his wife, Camille, on a beach.

Camille's white dress and blue parasol seem to glow in the sunshine, contrasting with her friend's dark outfit.

Sand in the paint shows the picture was actually painted on the beach.

The Beach at Trouville by Claude Monet, 1870

Impressions

The portraits on these pages were painted fast. The results are like quick snapshots or 'impressions' – and this style is known as Impressionism.

This study of a girl is flooded with light, probably from an unseen window. The light outlines her profile and lends vibrant touches of yellow, green, pink and white to her skin.

Study of a Girl's Head
by Edgar Degas, late 1870s

Berthe Morisot painted many portraits of friends and family, especially her daughter, Julie. This one shows Julie and her nanny in a local garden.

A Woman and Child in a Garden
(Julie Manet and her Nanny)
by Berthe Morisot, about 1883-84

A tree divides the scene down the middle, as if to emphasize the divide between the adult, busy with her sewing, and the child, gazing at her toy boat.

The natural poses and sketchy finish give Morisot's picture a casual feel, like a family snapshot. Notice how the brushstrokes get rougher and more blurry around the edges, helping to focus attention on the middle of the scene. You can even see brown patches of unpainted canvas.

This startled or fearful face belongs to artist Rembrandt van Rijn. Drawing his own face allowed him to study the expression without having to pay a model. It makes for an unusual portrait, but this sort of study was very useful when it came to painting scenes from stories.

Rembrandt made self portraits throughout his life. This dates from when he was 24.

Rembrandt pulls a dramatic expression, showing the whites of his eyes. Strong lighting adds to the drama.

Self Portrait
by Rembrandt van Rijn, 1630

Pulling faces

Most portraits show people smiling or looking serious, but some use different expressions to create striking effects.

This metal head is one of a series showing extreme expressions. It was probably based on the artist, but it isn't really a portrait. Instead, it's a study of how much a face can change with different expressions.

The Malicious One
by Franz Xaver Messerschmidt, after 1770

The Japanese print below shows a Japanese actor as he would look on stage, rolling his eyes and grimacing, in traditional stage make-up.

The actor's expression is exaggerated by his painted eyebrows, which stand out sharply against his whitened skin.

Artist Kunichika specialized in portraits of actors from popular plays.

Portrait of the actor Nakamura Shikan V, as Ishikawa Hachiemon
by Toyohara Kunichika, 1869

The portrait below was very progressive for its time, because of its informal, natural-looking poses. It shows three young sisters and an elderly servant enjoying a game of chess. It was painted by a fourth sister, Sofonisba, who went on to become court painter to the Queen of Spain.

The Chess Game
by Sofonisba Anguissola, 1555

At this time, chess was seen as a man's game, so it was unusual to show women playing.

Family

Before photographs, paintings were the only record families had of how their loved ones looked.

James Whistler's picture of his mother, Anna, uses a carefully limited range of colours. The dark colours help to create a feeling of seriousness, and focus attention on her delicately painted face and hands, framed by white lace.

Arrangement in Grey and Black No. 1
(The Artist's Mother)
by James Abbott McNeill Whistler, 1871

Notice the dog lying patiently at the girl's feet.

The girl in this picture is grasping a strawberry sprig. Flowers and fruit were often included with children as a symbol of growing up. Notice how her glowing red dress shows up against the dark background.

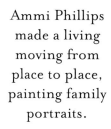

Ammi Phillips made a living moving from place to place, painting family portraits.

The same dog appears in several portraits by the same artist, so it may have belonged to him.

Portrait of a Girl in a Red Dress
by Ammi Phillips, 1830s

The self portrait on the left shows the poet and artist, Dante Gabriel Rossetti, aged 18, when he was still an art student. His wary, sideways glance and long, flowing hair present him just as he wished to be seen – as a rebellious, romantic spirit.

Self Portrait
by Dante Gabriel Rossetti, 1847

Self portraits

Many artists create self portraits, partly to perfect their skills, but also to advertise themselves to future clients.

Here, Parmigianino painted himself in a curved mirror. He captured the reflection with great accuracy, recording every distortion, as if to remind us how unreliable pictures can be. Notice how strange his hand looks, stretched by the curve.

Parmigianino gave his self portrait to the Pope – who hired him immediately.

Self Portrait
by Parmigianino,
about 1524

Elisabeth Vigée Le Brun made her name painting fashionable clients, including kings and queens. In this picture, she shows herself dressed as fashionably as any of them – an advertisement for her skills as an artist.

Le Brun grasps a palette and brushes – the tools of her trade – but would not really have worked in such fancy clothes.

Self Portrait in a Straw Hat by Elisabeth Vigée Le Brun, after 1782

The real-life details include fields of animals and a tower in the distance.

The tower belonged to the church where the couple married.

Gainsborough built model landscapes, with broccoli trees, to help him paint country scenes indoors.

Mr. and Mrs. Andrews

This double portrait of a wealthy young couple was probably painted to celebrate their marriage – and their newly acquired country estate in Suffolk, England.

Mr. Andrews poses with a gun and dog, as if about to set off hunting. By contrast, Mrs. Andrews wears a fancy silk dress and dainty indoor slippers. Notice the blank patch in her lap. It was meant to be filled in later, perhaps with a portrait of a hoped-for child.

It's an unusual arrangement for a portrait. The couple have been set to one side, giving pride of place to the lovingly detailed landscape. Although Gainsborough made his living from portraits, he said he preferred to paint landscapes – and this was one he knew especially well, having grown up nearby.

The couple sit beneath an oak tree, a traditional symbol of family, strength and stability. Beyond, the calmly grazing sheep and neat rows of corn are clear signs of a well-run estate. Mr. Andrews took a keen interest in farming, and may have asked the artist to include these details.

Mr. and Mrs. Andrews by Thomas Gainsborough, about 1750

This portrait shows the English poet, Lord Byron, wearing a gold-trimmed velvet costume from Albania. The foreign outfit showed viewers that he was an adventurous traveller. Byron had toured Albania and admired its clothes as 'the most magnificent in the world'.

George Gordon Byron, 6th Baron Byron
replica by Thomas Phillips, 1835 (copying a painting he originally made in 1813)

Dressing up

Some portraits show people dressed up as someone else – not just for fun, but to reveal something about their education or character.

The elder boy is dressed as the Greek hero Achilles.

Lockets like this often contained portraits of loved ones.

The boy on the right was painted as a winged cupid.

The Marquise de Seignelay and Two of her Sons
by Pierre Mignard, 1691

Here, a noblewoman poses as a Greek sea goddess, Thetis, adorned with pearls and coral, one foot resting on a shell. Notice her sad, thoughtful expression. The picture was painted soon after the death of her husband, an admiral, and the references to the sea are a tribute to him.

Fashion

It's not surprising if people like to be painted in their best clothes – but it can be surprising how much those clothes reveal.

When this was painted, enormous sleeves were all the fashion, partly due to a period of very cold weather.

Notice the letters 'TV' on the parapet – the initials of the artist, Tiziano Vecelli, known in English as Titian.

Portrait of a Man by Titian, about 1510

No one is quite sure who this man was. He might be a poet, a man named Gerolamo Barbarigo or even the artist himself. But his outfit, with huge, quilted silk sleeves, marks him out as both wealthy and stylish.

This picture of fashion designer Emilie Flöge was painted by her friend, Gustav Klimt, who covered it in rich mosaic patterns. The flowing style of Flöge's dress, as well as the decorative look of the painting itself, was ultra-modern at the time.

Flöge's loose dress was ground-breaking at a time when most women wore stiff corsets.

The 1970s portrait below shows the artist wearing an embroidered 'flower power' coat. Flower power was a movement that used flowers as symbols of peace and freedom.

Emilie Flöge by Gustav Klimt, 1902

Self Portrait in a Flowered Jacket
by John Byrne, 1971-73

Joseph Roulin

Joseph Roulin was a postal worker and friend of artist Vincent van Gogh, who painted his portrait several times.

Van Gogh also made portraits of Roulin's wife and children.

Self Portrait with Bandaged Ear
by Vincent van Gogh, 1889

Van Gogh met Roulin in Arles, a small town in France. Most of the locals thought Van Gogh was crazy, but Roulin admired his art and allowed Van Gogh to paint him. After Roulin moved away, Van Gogh dashed off the picture on the right from memory.

This self portrait of Van Gogh is from the same year. The bandage is because Van Gogh had cut off part of his ear while ill. Roulin tried to help him and visited him in hospital.

Van Gogh painted his friend – whom he described as 'such a good soul' – in a rich blue uniform, against a vivid green background. Van Gogh said he meant these glowing hues to suggest something spiritual, 'which the halo used to symbolize, which we seek to communicate by... colour.'

Portrait of Joseph Roulin by Vincent van Gogh, 1889

Before photographs, few ordinary people could afford a portrait. Paintings were too expensive. But silhouettes like the one on the left were a cheaper alternative. These were made by tracing around someone's shadow, recording an image in a way that anticipated photography.

Jane Austen
by an unknown artist,
about 1810-15

Photographs

The arrival of photography about 200 years ago changed portrait art forever.

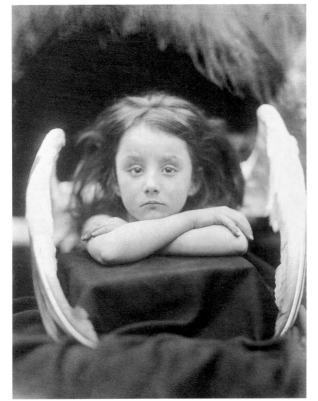

I Wait (Rachel Gurney)
by Julia Margaret Cameron, 1872

Julia Margaret Cameron was an early pioneer of portrait photography. She created dozens of portraits of her friends and family – often dressed as characters from stories, and arranged and lit as carefully as any painting.

Posing for early photographs meant staying *very* still.

Crude blocks of colour swamp this face, as if to highlight how fragile it is.

Liz by Andy Warhol, 1965

As photography became more widespread, artists began to experiment
with it – sometimes using photographs as the basis for other pictures.
In the 1960s, Andy Warhol used publicity photographs of celebrities to
create colourful prints, like this one of actress Elizabeth Taylor.

Lee Miller by Pablo Picasso, 1937

Different views

Some artists have taken the *idea* of painting a likeness, but gone a step further – as with the portrait opposite, by Pablo Picasso.

Self Portrait with Headband
by Lee Miller, about 1932

If you examine the features, you can see they were all painted from different angles. It's as if the sitter was constantly moving – just as people do in real life.

This is a photograph of Lee Miller, the woman in the painting. Try comparing the two images. Can you see a resemblance in the line of her profile and the shapes of her features?

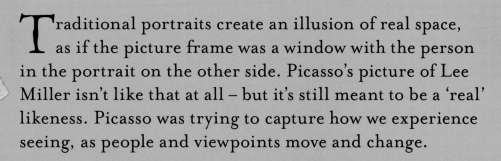

Mummy, mummy!

Traditional portraits create an illusion of real space, as if the picture frame was a window with the person in the portrait on the other side. Picasso's picture of Lee Miller isn't like that at all – but it's still meant to be a 'real' likeness. Picasso was trying to capture how we experience seeing, as people and viewpoints move and change.

When Lee Miller's two-year-old son saw the painting, he recognized her instantly.

'David' is a filmed portrait of football star David Beckham sleeping, by artist Sam Taylor-Johnson. The film was shot in one go, after a training session, without Beckham once waking up.

David Beckham ('David')
by Sam Taylor-Johnson, 2004

This is a still from the film – which lasts for 67 minute looping back to the beginning each time it reaches the en

By showing Beckham asleep, rather than focusing on the footballer's career or fame, Taylor-Wood creates a more gentle, personal portrait.

Portraits today

Artists today are finding new ways of making portraits, adapting new technologies and sometimes unusual materials to capture a likeness.

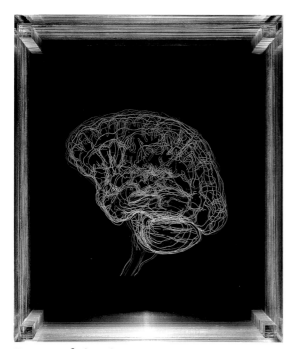

Brain of the Artist
by Angela Palmer, 2012

In this self portrait, a ghostly 3D outline hovers in space, engraved on 16 sheets of glass. The shape is that of the artist's brain, mapped with medical precision using a machine known as an MRI scanner.

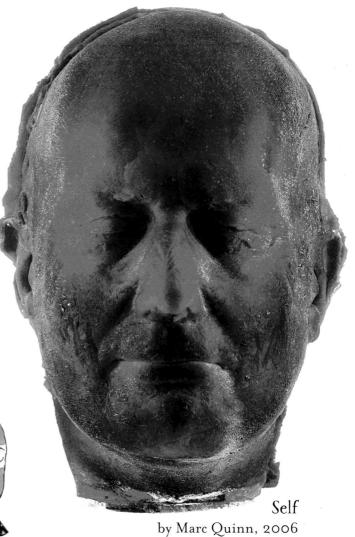

This striking sculpture shows the head of artist Marc Quinn, cast in frozen blood. The blood is Quinn's own, so the head represents not only how he looks, but his actual flesh and blood.

Self
by Marc Quinn, 2006

Casting the head

With help from assistants, Quinn greased his skin and coated his head with wet plaster. Once dry, the plaster made a hollow case.

He filled the case with blood and froze it. Then he opened the case, to reveal the finished head or 'cast'.

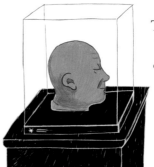

The head must be constantly chilled to stop it melting.

43

...and painting today

Artists continue to create portraits in paint – working in a huge range of styles and techniques.

Spanish artist Lita Cabellut has adapted a very old method of painting known as fresco, where you paint onto a layer of wet plaster.

People have been making fresco pictures since ancient times – usually by painting straight onto walls.

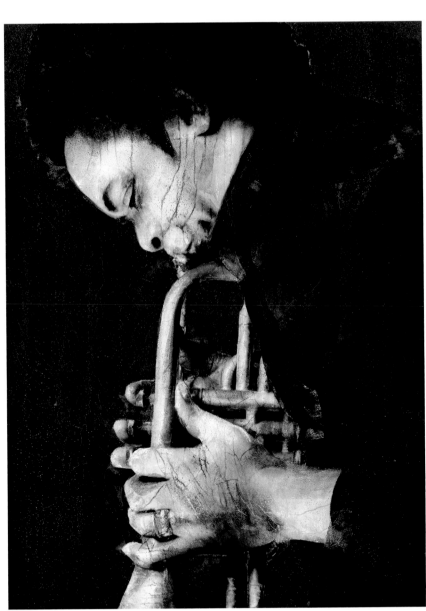

Miles Davis by Lita Cabellut, 2012

The fresco method gives Cabellut's portrait of a musician a very distinctive texture. Although painted in a lifelike way, you can see obvious smears and cracks – a deliberate effect – in the surface of the paint.

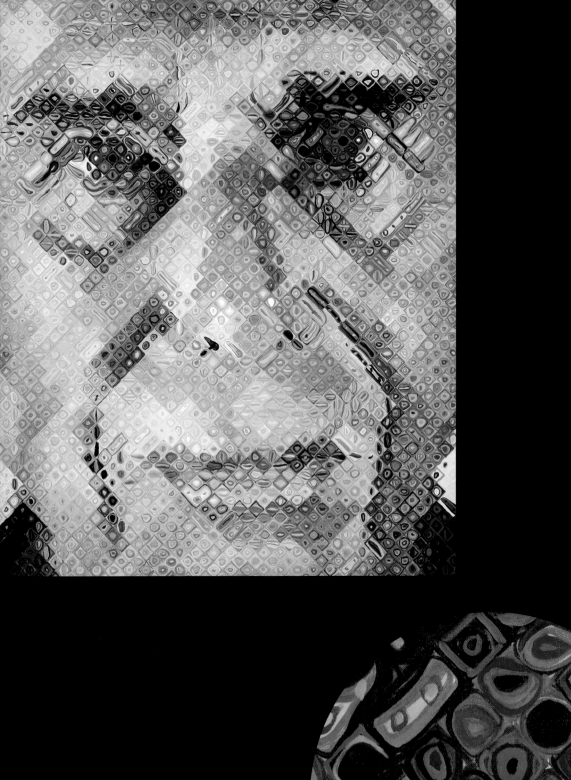
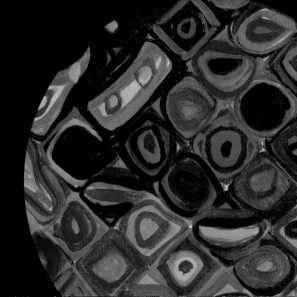

Timeline

Here, you can see how portraits developed and artists' techniques changed over time. You can also see where some of the portraits in this book fit in.

about 24,000 years ago
The earliest known images of faces are carved in bone.

The images were probably believed to have magical properties.

6,000-2,000 years ago
Early mirrors are made from polished stone or metal.

4,500 years ago
In ancient Egypt, portraits are created as part of preparations for the afterlife.

The 'fresco' method of painting over plaster is developed.

2,500 years ago
Art flourishes in ancient Greece. Portraits tend to be idealized.

2,200 years ago
In China, an army of terracotta soldiers is created.

1400s
Oil paints are developed, with ingredients prepared laboriously by hand.

Influenced by ancient art, portraits are often idealized, profile views.

about 1474-78
Leonardo paints Ginevra de' Benci, helping to popularize the three-quarter view.

1500s
Glass mirrors are invented, making it much easier to create a self portrait.

1650s
Oliver Cromwell is said to have demanded his portrait show him 'warts and all'.

1700s
Some artists set up studios specializing in fashionable portraits.

Ready-made paints start to be sold in shops.

1750
Gainsborough paints *Mr. and Mrs. Andrews.*

1835
Good-quality mirrors become widely available, thanks to a new method of glass making.

1838
Early photographs known as 'daguerreotypes' are invented.

1840s
Many bright new chemical paint colours are discovered. Metal paint tubes are invented.

1870s
Julia Margaret Cameron experiments with early 'glass-plate' photographs.

Monet and other 'Impressionist' painters experiment with a rougher, less polished style of painting.

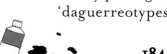

1880s
New kinds of cameras start to be sold. Using light-sensitive film, they make photography much cheaper and easier.

1889
Van Gogh paints *Joseph Roulin* – and the rest of the Roulin family.

1892
Singer Sargent paints *Lady Agnew of Lochnaw.*

1907
Picasso and other 'Cubist' artists try combining views from different points in the same picture.

1937
Picasso paints *Lee Miller.*

1965
Warhol creates his print, *Liz.*

1970s
Digital cameras are invented.

2000s
As well as painting, portrait artists experiment with everything from brain scans to blood.

Acknowledgements

Editorial director: Jane Chisholm.
Art director: Mary Cartwright. Digital manipulation by John Russell.

Cover: *Mr. and Mrs. Andrews*, see credits for pages 30-31. *Lady Agnew of Lochnaw*, see credits for pages 14-15. *George Gordon Byron, 6th Baron Byron*, see credits for pages 32-33. **Pages 2-3:** *Portrait of the actor Nakamura Shikan V*, see credits for pages 24-25. **Pages 4-5:** *Girl with a Pearl Earring* (c.1665) by Johannes Vermeer © Archivart/Alamy Stock Photo. *Sir Walter Ralegh (also spelled Raleigh)* (c.1585) by Nicholas Hilliard © National Portrait Gallery, London. *Self Portrait with Monkey* (1938) by Frida Kahlo, Albright Knox Art Gallery/Art Resource, NY/Scala, Florence © Banco de México Diego Rivera Frida Kahlo Museums Trust, Mexico, D.F./DACS 2016. *Queen of Scots, Sovereign of the Most Ancient and Most Noble Order of the Thistle and Chief of the Chiefs* (photographed 2010, printed 2013) by Julian Calder, National Galleries of Scotland © Julian Calder. **Pages 6-7:** *Woman from Brassempouy* (c.24,000 years ago), DeAgostini Picture Library/Scala, Florence. *Terracotta Soldier* (3rd century BCE), Best View Stock/Alamy Stock Photo. *Mask of Tutankhamun* (c.1323 BCE) © REX/Shutterstock. *A Man with a Wreath* (c.2nd-3rd century CE) by an unknown Egyptian artist © The National Gallery, London. **Pages 8-9:** *Alexander the Great as Apollo* (gold coin known as a 'stater', c.322 BCE), photo courtesy the Colosseo Collection. *Charioteer of Delphi* (c.478-474 BCE), DeAgostini Picture Library/Scala, Florence. *Portrait of a Lady* (c.1465) by Alesso Baldovinetti © The National Gallery, London. **Pages 10-11:** *Ginevra de' Benci* (c.1474-78) by Leonardo da Vinci, National Gallery of Art, Washington DC © Archivart/Alamy Stock Photo. *Wreath of Laurel, Palm and Juniper with a Scroll* (1478) by Leonardo da Vinci, Smithsonian National Gallery of Art © B. Christopher/Alamy Stock Photo. **Pages 12-13:** *Oliver Cromwell* (1656) by Samuel Cooper © National Portrait Gallery, London. *An Old Woman ('The Ugly Duchess')* (c.1513) by Quinten Massys © The National Gallery, London. *The Duchess and her Family* (1891) by John Tenniel (coloured by Emily Gertrude Thompson) © AF Fotografie/Alamy Stock Photo. *An Old Man and his Grandson* (c.1490) by Domenico Ghirlandaio, photo © RMN-Grand Palais (Musée du Louvre)/Hervé Lewandowski. **Pages 14-15:** *Study for a Portrait of Horace Walpole* (c.1759) by Allan Ramsay © National Galleries of Scotland. *Mary Robinson* (c.1782) by Sir Joshua Reynolds © National Portrait Gallery, London. *Louise de Broglie, Countess of Haussonville* (1842) by Jean-Auguste-Dominique Ingres, Musée Bonnat, Bayonne, France/Bridgeman Images. **Pages 16-17:** *King George IV* (c.1814) by Sir Thomas Lawrence © National Portrait Gallery, London. *Lady Agnew of Lochnaw* (1892) by John Singer Sargent © National Galleries of Scotland. **Pages 18-19:** *Shah Jahan seated on the Peacock Throne* (c.1635) by Govardhan, Pictures from History/Bridgeman Images. *Head of a Yoruba Queen* (600-900 years ago), Pictures from History/Bridgeman Images. *Mary I* (1544) by Master John © National Portrait Gallery, London. **Pages 20-21:** *The Lacemaker* (c.1669-70) by Johannes Vermeer, Louvre, Paris, France/Bridgeman Images. *Portrait of a Man* and *Portrait of a Woman* (c.1435) by Robert Campin © The National Gallery, London. **Pages 22-23:** *Beach at Trouville* (1870) by Claude Monet © The National Gallery, London. *Study of a Girl's Head* (late 1870s) by Edgar Degas © National Galleries of Scotland. *A Woman and Child in a Garden (Julie Manet and her Nanny)* (c.1883-84) by Berthe Morisot © National Galleries of Scotland. **Pages 24-25:** *Self Portrait* (1630) by Rembrandt van Rijn, Private Collection/Bridgeman Images. *The Malicious One* (after 1770) by Franz Xaver Messerschmidt © Peter Willi/Superstock. *Portrait of the actor Nakamura Shikan V, as Ishikawa Hachiemon* (pub. 1869) by Toyohara Kunichika, British Library, London © British Library Board, All Rights Reserved/Bridgeman Images. **Pages 26-27:** *The Chess Game* (1555) by Sofonisba Anguissola, Museum Narodowe, Poznan, Poland/Bridgeman Images. *Arrangement in Grey and Black No. 1 (The Artist's Mother)* (1871) by James Abbott McNeill Whistler, Musée D'Orsay, Paris © Peter Barritt/Alamy Stock Photo. *Portrait of a Girl in a Red Dress* (1830s) by Ammi Phillips, photo © Christie's Images/Bridgeman Images. **Pages 28-29:** *Self Portrait* (1847) by Dante Gabriel Rossetti © National Portrait Gallery, London. *Self Portrait at the Mirror* (c.1524) by Parmigianino, Kunsthistorisches Museum, Vienna, Austria/Ali Meyer/Bridgeman Images. *Self Portrait in a Straw Hat* (after 1782) by Elisabeth Vigée Le Brun © The National Gallery, London. **Pages 30-31:** *Mr. and Mrs. Andrews* (c.1750) by Thomas Gainsborough © The National Gallery, London. **Pages 32-33:** *George Gordon Byron, 6th Baron Byron* (1835 replica of 1813 original) by Thomas Phillips © National Portrait Gallery, London. *The Marquise de Seignelay and Two of her Sons* (1691) by Pierre Mignard © The National Gallery, London. **Pages 34-35:** *Portrait of a Man, possibly Gerolamo Barbarigo* (c.1510) by Titian © The National Gallery, London. *Emilie Flöge* (1902) by Gustav Klimt © classicpaintings/Alamy Stock Photo. *Self Portrait in a Flowered Jacket* (1971-73) by John Byrne © National Galleries of Scotland © John Byrne, All Rights Reserved, DACS 2016. **Pages 36-37:** *Self Portrait with Bandaged Ear* (1889) by Vincent van Gogh © REX/Shutterstock. *Portrait of Joseph Roulin* (1889) by Vincent van Gogh, Museum of Modern Art, New York, USA/Bridgeman Images. **Pages 38-39:** *Jane Austen* (1810-15) © National Portrait Gallery, London. *I Wait (Rachel Gurney)* (1872) by Julia Margaret Cameron, Artokoloro Quint Lox Limited/Alamy Stock Photo. *Liz* (1965) by Andy Warhol, photo © National Galleries of Scotland, © 2016 The Andy Warhol Foundation for the Visual Arts, Inc./Artists Rights Society (ARS), New York and DACS, London 2016. **Pages 40-41:** *Lee Miller* (1937) by Pablo Picasso, photo © National Galleries of Scotland, © Succession Picasso/DACS, London 2016. *Self Portrait with Headband, New York Studio, USA* (c.1932) by Lee Miller, photo © National Galleries of Scotland, © Lee Miller Archives, England 2016, All Rights Reserved, www.leemiller.co.uk **Pages 42-43:** *David Beckham ('David')* (2004) film by Sam Taylor-Johnson, photo © National Portrait Gallery, London, © Sam Taylor-Johnson, All Rights Reserved, DACS 2016. *Brain of the Artist* (2012) by Angela Palmer, photo © National Galleries of Scotland, with kind permission © Angela Palmer. *Self* (2006) by Marc Quinn, photo © National Portrait Gallery, London, with kind permission © Marc Quinn. **Pages 44-45:** *Miles Davis* (2012) by Lita Cabellut, with kind permission © Lita Cabellut. *Paul III* (1996) by Chuck Close, oil on canvas, 259 x 213cm (102 x 84in), The Cleveland Museum of Art, Mr. and Mrs. William H. Marlatt Fund 1997.59 © Chuck Close, photograph by Ellen Page Wilson, courtesy The Pace Gallery.

First published in 2017 by Usborne Publishing Ltd., Usborne House,
83-85 Saffron Hill, London EC1N 8RT, England. www.usborne.com